My Sweet 15 Planner

Beatriz Cantu

My Sweet 15 Planner

Cover Design by Marco Alvarez
Layout by LDG Juan Manuel Serna Rosales

Printed in the United States of America
ISBN: 9781957058610
LCCN: 2022912656

My Quinceañera Planner

....

Date and time

....

Location of party

....

Church

....

Church Ceremony:

Start Time: _____

End Time: _____

Reception:

Start Time: _____

End Time: _____

Dedication

I want to dedicate this *Quinceañera Planner* mainly to my daughter Ashlee and to each and every one of those quinceañeras that God has placed in my life that I have been able to help and motivate throughout my career with my magazine. There have been so many young girls, so many stories that have impacted my life but without a doubt each one has left a valuable lesson and great memories. Thanks for being a part of my life.

Introduction

Turning fifteen is a major milestone in a girl's life and planning your Quinceañera is one of the most exciting things you will ever do. We know how stressful can be to plan a Quinceañera, but if you stay on track by following this amazing *My Sweet 15 Planner*, you'll find that planning can be fun too! The most important thing is to remember to have fun and enjoy your party.

TABLE OF **CONTENTS**

Why is my Quinceañera important?

Before you begin planning your party, answer these questions below to understand the importance of having a Quinceañera.

What does turning fifteen mean to you?

_____
_____
_____
_____
_____
_____

Why is it important for you to have a Quinceañera?

_____
_____
_____
_____
_____
_____

What do you wish to learn from turning fifteen?

_____
_____
_____
_____
_____

Quince
Timeline

Quince Timeline

Planning your Quince party can be easier when you have a timeline to follow. Follow this step-by- step guide and enjoy your party from first day to the last!

12 MONTHS BEFORE DATE_____

- ☐ Consider possible event dates
- ☐ Research reception venues
- ☐ Contact the church priest
- ☐ Figure out your budget
- ☐ Start your guest list
- ☐ Choose a theme and color scheme
- ☐ Set date
- ☐ Book your venue and church
- ☐ Select potential Godparents
- ☐ Go to Expo 15
- ☐ Go and get Sweet 15 Magazine

9 MONTHS BEFORE DATE_____

- ☐ Research Quinceanera dresses
- ☐ Decide your Quince court
- ☐ Hire a DJ and music
- ☐ Research invitation designs
- ☐ Hire choreographer
- ☐ Plan de vals and baile sorpresa
- ☐ Select your dress
- ☐ Select makeup and hair stylists
- ☐ Reserve hotel blocks for out-of-town guests
- ☐ Choose attire for your quince court

6 MONTHS BEFORE DATE_____

- ☐ Create and order your save the date
- ☐ Schedule a portrait photo session
- ☐ Research florist, decor ideas
- ☐ Choose the last doll
- ☐ Order Invitations
- ☐ Order Damas dresses
- ☐ Fit Chambelanes for tuxedo
- ☐ Select menu
- ☐ Book transportation

3 MONTHS BEFORE DATE_____

- ☐ Send save the date
- ☐ Final dress fitting
- ☐ Hair and Makeup trial
- ☐ Order cake
- ☐ Order party favors
- ☐ Schedule dance rehearsals
- ☐ Finalize food menu
- ☐ Shop for accessories
- ☐ Shop for shoes

My Sweet 15 Planner

1 MONTH BEFORE   DATE_____

- [ ] Rehearsal dance with dad
- [ ] Confirm all reservations
- [ ] Confirm music selection
- [ ] Chose host/MC
- [ ] Send out invitations
- [ ] Write speeches
- [ ] Plan music playlists
- [ ] Create seating plan
- [ ] Share the seating plan with venue

1 WEEK BEFORE   DATE_____

- [ ] Confirm details with all your vendors
- [ ] Wrap gifts for padrinos, parents and court
- [ ] Pay all providers
- [ ] Confirm Hotel block
- [ ] Confirm with cake decorator
- [ ] Pick up the dress
- [ ] Give music list to DJ
- [ ] Keep practicing dances

1 DAY BEFORE   DATE_____

- [ ] Pull together any last-minute essentials
- [ ] Get ready to enjoy your big day.

IT'S TODAY!   DATE_____

Enjoy your big day!

My Quinceanera Budget

	BUDGET	TOTAL COST	PADRINOS	CONTRIBUTION	BALANCE
Venue					
Church fees					
Invitations					
Dress					
Hairstyle and Makeup					
Choreography					
Catering					
Music/ DJ					
Decoration					
Cake					
Dessert Table					
Photography and video					
Photo booth					
Limo					
Quince Shoes					
Jewelry					
Nails					
Tiara					
Security					

Padrinos y
Madrinas

Padrinos and Madrinas List

Phone	Name

Padrinos and Madrinas List

Phone	Name

Padrinos and Madrinas List

Phone	Name

Dress

Dress
Find the perfect style for your Quinceañera

Choosing the best dress is your priority. I have always said that the most important part for a girl when planning a Quinceañera party is her dress.

When it comes to styles and colors, the truth is that there are no designs that are specifically trending. Since all quinceañeras want to be unique, each girl has a different taste in color and theme. It could be a charro, rustic, elegant, charming party or simply a simple party. No matter the color or style, what matters most is that you like your dress. That is the best choice you make since all quinceañeras are beautiful in her own way.

Choosing the perfect dress will depend on what color suits your skin tone. With each color you try on, you will notice a change since not all of us have the same skin tone; they are all different. You could have a color in mind and when you try it on, you will see that it does not suit your skin well and that is fine since this happens to many girls.

So I advise you to keep an open mind when shopping. The style of quinceañera dress differs more than anything in that if it will have ruffles or you want it with glitter or not. Don't be afraid to tell the store if you don't like a dress, do not feel obligated to like it. Remember: This is the most important decision of your party that you will have to make and it has to be the perfect dress for you!

If you have already chosen your dress, then all that is left to do is to make sure that the dress fits you well. Most dresses already come with a built-in bra but if it doesn't, make sure you have the right undergarments for your dress.

Once you have your dress, a very important part is that the length is perfect. You do not want to end up dragging your dress all night. It's a big night and your dress shouldn't get in the way of anything. How do you know if it's the perfect length for you? You will know when you leave the dressing room and you can turn around 2 times without any problem and walk from side to side without tripping. One piece of advice that I always like to give is to measure your dress without shoes and if that way you don't trip, then you have the perfect length for your dress.

In case your dress is too long, ask for another crinoline, maybe one of tulle above the wire one to be able to lift it a little but I warn you that when we use a second crinoline we make the dress a little more fluffy. This is a more effective solution before thinking about trimming and fitting the dress.

Isabel Hernandez
Vestidos Couture

f Vestidos Couture   Vestidos Couture

Vestido COUTURE

Dress Checklist

Style: _____

Color: _____

Fabric: _____

BOUTIQUE OR DESIGNER

Location: _____

Contact: _____

Email: _____

Price $: _____

Date to schedule visit: _____

Time: _____

Style: _____

Color: _____

Fabric: _____

BOUTIQUE OR DESIGNER

Location: _____

Contact: _____

Email: _____

Price $: _____

Date to schedule visit: _____

Time: _____

Style: _____

Color: _____

Fabric: _____

BOUTIQUE OR DESIGNER

Location: _____

Contact: _____

Email: _____

Price $: _____

Date to schedule visit: _____

Time: _____

Style: _____

Color: _____

Fabric: _____

BOUTIQUE OR DESIGNER

Location: _____

Contact: _____

Email: _____

Price $: _____

Date to schedule visit: _____

Time: _____

Shoes

Choosing the perfect pair of shoes is important to be comfortable during your Quince party.

1. Choose your style
2. Heel height
3. Choose your color
4. Choose your shoes fabric

Don't forget extra shoes for after your quince.

Now is time to choose the perfect crystal, flower crown or headdress for you.

I recommend that when you make this decision you have your dress, either on or with you, since it is important to ensure that all accessories such as chokers, earrings, and slippers match the design details and glassware of your dress.

Congratulations, now you have everything you need for your big day in terms of your trousseau

Makeup and Hairstyle

MAKEUP

1. Pick the perfect professional makeup artist
2. Choose your makeup look
3. Book makeup trial
4. Book makeup appointment for the day of

HAIRSTYLE

1. Think about your Quince dress. Which hairstyle would match it best?
2. Updo? Down? Half up-Half down?
3. Will you have accessories in your hair?
4. Is it comfortable?
5. Book Hair Trial

Makeup and Hairstyle

HAIRSTYLIST

Location: _____

Contact:_____

Email: _____

Date: _____

MAKEUP TRIAL

Salon:_____

Location: _____

Contact:_____

Email:_____

Date: _____

Time: _____

Venue

The venue for your special day is the most important after your dress.
Follow this guide to make sure you are covering all the details.

1. Accessibility
2. Accommodation
3. Timing
4. Pricing
5. Parking

Venue Checklist

Name of venue: _____

Address/Area:_____

Style: _____

Parking availability: _____

Seating Capacity: _____

Green rooms: _____

Distance from Church: _____

Availability

XV date available?   _____Yes   _____No

Optional dates _____

_____

_____

Pricing

Venue cost: $_____

Cost per head range: $_____

Price includes:

- Buffet $_____
- Venue & catering   _____Yes _____No

If no, extra fee for exclusive caterer

Price $_____

- Cash Bar   _____Yes _____No
- Open Bar   _____Yes _____No
- Just Venue   _____Yes _____No

If no, extra fee for alternative

Price $_____

- Linen   _____Yes _____No

If no, extra fee for linen

Price$_____

- Security   _____Yes _____No

If no, extra fee for security

Price: $_____

- Cleaning   _____Yes _____ No

If no, extra fee for cleaning

Price: $_____

Is there a reception cut-off time?

_____Yes _____No

Rate per hour: $_____

Security Deposit: $_____

Notes: _____

_____

_____

_____

_____

_____

_____

_____

_____

_____

_____

_____

_____

_____

_____

_____

Church Ceremony

1. Anticipated time to reserve the church.
2. Check which sacraments the church requires the Quinceañera to have in order to hold the Mass. Many churches require you to be baptized and have to your First Communion.
3. Preparatory class: Many churches have the Quinceañera attend a class to teach them the significance of turning 15.
4. Determine the fee for the Mass.
5. Restrictions on decorations vary with every church. Checking what the church allows is important to avoid any problems the day of.

Church Ceremony Checklist

Quinceañera Date:

CEREMONY TIME: _____

Ceremony location: _____

Name: _____

Address: _____

Contact person: _____

Phone: _____

Email: _____

Musicians: _____

Name: _____

Contact: _____

Song selection: _____

Church decorations: _____

Name: _____

Contact: _____

Rehearsal: _____

Date : _____

Time: _____

Photographer: _____

Name: _____

Contact: _____

Decorations

Decorations

1. Define your theme
   Can be Charro, princess, masquerade, carnival, beach and more.
2. The main table
   This is the table where you and your court will be seated
3. Quince Centerpieces
4. Tablecloths

Make sure everything looks impeccable

Theme of my XV

....

Main Table

Table Decorations:
_____
_____

Chambelanes:
_____

Damas:
_____

Quince Centerpieces

Quantity: _____

Price: _____

Supplier: _____

Tablecloths

Size: _____

Quantity: _____

Supplier: _____

Choose your table dimensions, sizes, and seats

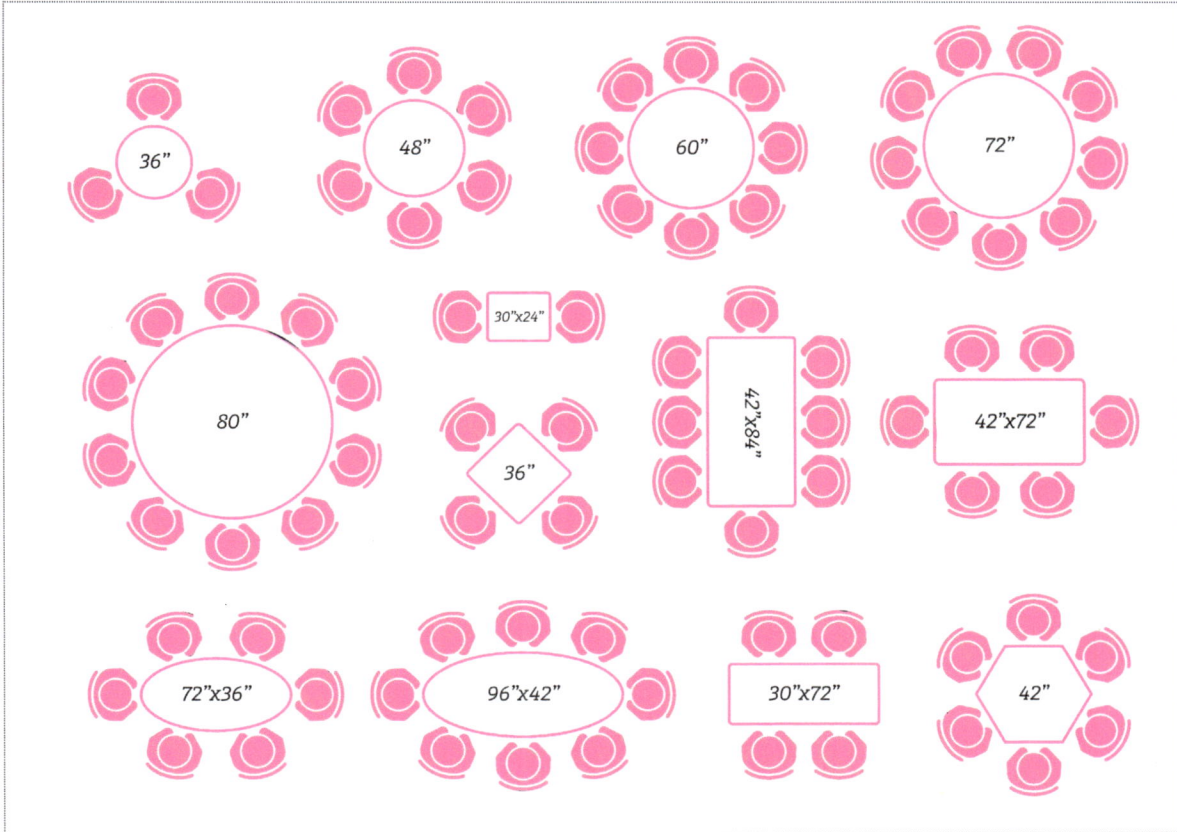

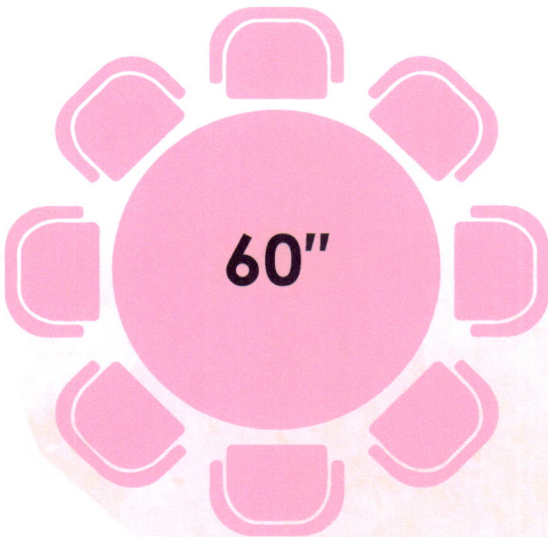

36"

48"

60"

72"

80"

30"x24"

36"

42"x84"

42"x72"

72"x36"

96"x42"

30"x72"

42"

60"

Seat 1 ....

Seat 2 ....

Seat 3 ....

Seat 4 ....

Seat 5 ....

Seat 6 ....

Seat 7 ....

Seat 8 ....

Seat 1
Seat 2
Seat 3
Seat 4
Seat 5
Seat 6
Seat 7
Seat 8

Table #
_____

Seat 1
Seat 2
Seat 3
Seat 4
Seat 5
Seat 6
Seat 7
Seat 8

Table #
_____

Seat 1
Seat 2
Seat 3
Seat 4
Seat 5
Seat 6
Seat 7
Seat 8

Table #
_____

Seat 1
Seat 2
Seat 3
Seat 4
Seat 5
Seat 6
Seat 7
Seat 8

Table #
_____

Seat 1
Seat 2
Seat 3
Seat 4
Seat 5
Seat 6
Seat 7
Seat 8

Table #
_____

Seat 1
Seat 2
Seat 3
Seat 4
Seat 5
Seat 6
Seat 7
Seat 8

Table #
_____

Dimensions

Tables
Sizes
Chairs

Notes

Seat 1 ....
Seat 2 ....
Seat 3 ....
Seat 4 ....
Seat 5 ....
Seat 6 ....
Seat 7 ....
Seat 8 ....

Table #
_____

Seat 1 ....
Seat 2 ....
Seat 3 ....
Seat 4 ....
Seat 5 ....
Seat 6 ....
Seat 7 ....
Seat 8 ....

Table #
_____

Seat 1 ....
Seat 2 ....
Seat 3 ....
Seat 4 ....
Seat 5 ....
Seat 6 ....
Seat 7 ....
Seat 8 ....

Table #
_____

Seat 1 ....
Seat 2 ....
Seat 3 ....
Seat 4 ....
Seat 5 ....
Seat 6 ....
Seat 7 ....
Seat 8 ....

Table #
_____

Seat 1 ....
Seat 2 ....
Seat 3 ....
Seat 4 ....
Seat 5 ....
Seat 6 ....
Seat 7 ....
Seat 8 ....

Table #
_____

Seat 1 ....
Seat 2 ....
Seat 3 ....
Seat 4 ....
Seat 5 ....
Seat 6 ....
Seat 7 ....
Seat 8 ....

Table #
_____

Dimensions

Tables ....
Sizes ....
Chairs ....

Notes

Seat 1 ....
Seat 2 ....
Seat 3 ....
Seat 4 ....
Seat 5 ....
Seat 6 ....
Seat 7 ....
Seat 8 ....

Table #
_____

Seat 1 ....
Seat 2 ....
Seat 3 ....
Seat 4 ....
Seat 5 ....
Seat 6 ....
Seat 7 ....
Seat 8 ....

Table #
_____

Seat 1 ....
Seat 2 ....
Seat 3 ....
Seat 4 ....
Seat 5 ....
Seat 6 ....
Seat 7 ....
Seat 8 ....

Table #
_____

Seat 1 ....
Seat 2 ....
Seat 3 ....
Seat 4 ....
Seat 5 ....
Seat 6 ....
Seat 7 ....
Seat 8 ....

Table #
_____

Seat 1 ....
Seat 2 ....
Seat 3 ....
Seat 4 ....
Seat 5 ....
Seat 6 ....
Seat 7 ....
Seat 8 ....

Table #
_____

Seat 1 ....
Seat 2 ....
Seat 3 ....
Seat 4 ....
Seat 5 ....
Seat 6 ....
Seat 7 ....
Seat 8 ....

Table #
_____

Dimensions

Tables ....
Sizes ....
Chairs ....

Notes

....
....
....
....
....

Seat 1 ....
Seat 2 ....
Seat 3 ....
Seat 4 ....
Seat 5 ....
Seat 6 ....
Seat 7 ....
Seat 8 ....

Table #
_____

Seat 1 ....
Seat 2 ....
Seat 3 ....
Seat 4 ....
Seat 5 ....
Seat 6 ....
Seat 7 ....
Seat 8 ....

Table #
_____

Seat 1 ....
Seat 2 ....
Seat 3 ....
Seat 4 ....
Seat 5 ....
Seat 6 ....
Seat 7 ....
Seat 8 ....

Table #
_____

Seat 1 ....
Seat 2 ....
Seat 3 ....
Seat 4 ....
Seat 5 ....
Seat 6 ....
Seat 7 ....
Seat 8 ....

Table #
_____

Seat 1 ....
Seat 2 ....
Seat 3 ....
Seat 4 ....
Seat 5 ....
Seat 6 ....
Seat 7 ....
Seat 8 ....

Table #
_____

Seat 1 ....
Seat 2 ....
Seat 3 ....
Seat 4 ....
Seat 5 ....
Seat 6 ....
Seat 7 ....
Seat 8 ....

Table #
_____

Dimensions

Tables ....
Sizes ....
Chairs ....

Notes

Is Your Court Present?

Chambelan of Honor: _____

Damas	Chambelanes
Name:_____	**Name:**_____
Present? YES___ NO___	Present? YES___ NO___
Name:_____	**Name:**_____
Present? YES___ NO___	Present? YES___ NO___
Name:_____	**Name:**_____
Present? YES___ NO___	Present? YES___ NO___
Name:_____	**Name:**_____
Present? YES___ NO___	Present? YES___ NO___
Name:_____	**Name:**_____
Present? YES___ NO___	Present? YES___ NO___
Name:_____	**Name:**_____
Present? YES___ NO___	Present? YES___ NO___
Name:_____	**Name:**_____
Present? YES___ NO___	Present? YES___ NO___
Name:_____	**Name:**_____
Present? YES___ NO___	Present? YES___ NO___
Name:_____	**Name:**_____
Present? YES___ NO___	Present? YES___ NO___
Name:_____	**Name:**_____
Present? YES___ NO___	Present? YES___ NO___

Your Court of Honor

Damas	Chambelanes

Chambelan of Honor: _____

Court Contact Information

NAME: ....

Phone Number: ....
Parent's Number: ....
Dress / Suit Size: ....
Shirt Size: ....
Shoe Size: ....

NAME: ....

Phone Number: ....
Parent's Number: ....
Dress / Suit Size: ....
Shirt Size: ....
Shoe Size: ....

NAME: ....

Phone Number: ....
Parent's Number: ....
Dress / Suit Size: ....
Shirt Size: ....
Shoe Size: ....

NAME: ....

Phone Number: ....
Parent's Number: ....
Dress / Suit Size: ....
Shirt Size: ....
Shoe Size: ....

NAME: ....

Phone Number: ....
Parent's Number: ....
Dress / Suit Size: ....
Shirt Size: ....
Shoe Size: ....

NAME: ....

Phone Number: ....
Parent's Number: ....
Dress / Suit Size: ....
Shirt Size: ....
Shoe Size: ....

NAME: ....

Phone Number: ....
Parent's Number: ....
Dress / Suit Size: ....
Shirt Size: ....
Shoe Size: ....

NAME: ....

Phone Number: ....
Parent's Number: ....
Dress / Suit Size: ....
Shirt Size: ....
Shoe Size: ....

Court Contact Information

NAME: ....

Phone Number: ....
Parent's Number: ....
Dress / Suit Size: ....
Shirt Size: ....
Shoe Size: ....

NAME: ....

Phone Number: ....
Parent's Number: ....
Dress / Suit Size: ....
Shirt Size: ....
Shoe Size: ....

NAME: ....

Phone Number: ....
Parent's Number: ....
Dress / Suit Size: ....
Shirt Size: ....
Shoe Size: ....

NAME: ....

Phone Number: ....
Parent's Number: ....
Dress / Suit Size: ....
Shirt Size: ....
Shoe Size: ....

NAME: ....

Phone Number: ....
Parent's Number: ....
Dress / Suit Size: ....
Shirt Size: ....
Shoe Size: ....

NAME: ....

Phone Number: ....
Parent's Number: ....
Dress / Suit Size: ....
Shirt Size: ....
Shoe Size: ....

NAME: ....

Phone Number: ....
Parent's Number: ....
Dress / Suit Size: ....
Shirt Size: ....
Shoe Size: ....

NAME: ....

Phone Number: ....
Parent's Number: ....
Dress / Suit Size: ....
Shirt Size: ....
Shoe Size: ....

Court Contact Information

NAME: ....

Phone Number: ....
Parent's Number: ....
Dress / Suit Size: ....
Shirt Size: ....
Shoe Size: ....

NAME: ....

Phone Number: ....
Parent's Number: ....
Dress / Suit Size: ....
Shirt Size: ....
Shoe Size: ....

NAME: ....

Phone Number: ....
Parent's Number: ....
Dress / Suit Size: ....
Shirt Size: ....
Shoe Size: ....

NAME: ....

Phone Number: ....
Parent's Number: ....
Dress / Suit Size: ....
Shirt Size: ....
Shoe Size: ....

NAME: ....

Phone Number: ....
Parent's Number: ....
Dress / Suit Size: ....
Shirt Size: ....
Shoe Size: ....

NAME: ....

Phone Number: ....
Parent's Number: ....
Dress / Suit Size: ....
Shirt Size: ....
Shoe Size: ....

NAME: ....

Phone Number: ....
Parent's Number: ....
Dress / Suit Size: ....
Shirt Size: ....
Shoe Size: ....

NAME: ....

Phone Number: ....
Parent's Number: ....
Dress / Suit Size: ....
Shirt Size: ....
Shoe Size: ....

Court Contact Information

NAME: ....

Phone Number: ....
Parent's Number: ....
Dress / Suit Size: ....
Shirt Size: ....
Shoe Size: ....

NAME: ....

Phone Number: ....
Parent's Number: ....
Dress / Suit Size: ....
Shirt Size: ....
Shoe Size: ....

NAME: ....

Phone Number: ....
Parent's Number: ....
Dress / Suit Size: ....
Shirt Size: ....
Shoe Size: ....

NAME: ....

Phone Number: ....
Parent's Number: ....
Dress / Suit Size: ....
Shirt Size: ....
Shoe Size: ....

NAME: ....

Phone Number: ....
Parent's Number: ....
Dress / Suit Size: ....
Shirt Size: ....
Shoe Size: ....

NAME: ....

Phone Number: ....
Parent's Number: ....
Dress / Suit Size: ....
Shirt Size: ....
Shoe Size: ....

NAME: ....

Phone Number: ....
Parent's Number: ....
Dress / Suit Size: ....
Shirt Size: ....
Shoe Size: ....

NAME: ....

Phone Number: ....
Parent's Number: ....
Dress / Suit Size: ....
Shirt Size: ....
Shoe Size: ....

Guest List

Remember invite the people that are important to you and your parents.
Follow these tips:

1. Think about the budget
   Define your budget before planning how big you want your quinceanera to be.
2. Set your priorities
3. Make your guest list

Family Guest List

FAMILY	ADDRESS	PHONE	#TABLE	Invitation sent	RSVP'd
				☐	☐
				☐	☐
				☐	☐
				☐	☐
				☐	☐
				☐	☐
				☐	☐
				☐	☐
				☐	☐
				☐	☐
				☐	☐
				☐	☐
				☐	☐
				☐	☐
				☐	☐
				☐	☐
				☐	☐
				☐	☐
				☐	☐

Family Guest List

FAMILY	ADDRESS	PHONE	#TABLE	Invitation sent	RSVP'd
				☐	☐
				☐	☐
				☐	☐
				☐	☐
				☐	☐
				☐	☐
				☐	☐
				☐	☐
				☐	☐
				☐	☐
				☐	☐
				☐	☐
				☐	☐
				☐	☐
				☐	☐
				☐	☐
				☐	☐
				☐	☐
				☐	☐

Family Guest List

FAMILY	ADDRESS	PHONE	#TABLE	Invitation sent	RSVP'd
				☐	☐
				☐	☐
				☐	☐
				☐	☐
				☐	☐
				☐	☐
				☐	☐
				☐	☐
				☐	☐
				☐	☐
				☐	☐
				☐	☐
				☐	☐
				☐	☐
				☐	☐
				☐	☐
				☐	☐
				☐	☐
				☐	☐

Family Guest List

FAMILY	ADDRESS	PHONE	#TABLE	Invitation sent	RSVP'd
				☐	☐
				☐	☐
				☐	☐
				☐	☐
				☐	☐
				☐	☐
				☐	☐
				☐	☐
				☐	☐
				☐	☐
				☐	☐
				☐	☐
				☐	☐
				☐	☐
				☐	☐
				☐	☐
				☐	☐
				☐	☐
				☐	☐

Personal Guest List

NAME: ....

Address: ....
Phone: ....
Email: ....
#Table: ....

Invitation sent?   YES ☐   NO ☐

NAME: ....

Address: ....
Phone: ....
Email: ....
#Table: ....

Invitation sent?   YES ☐   NO ☐

NAME: ....

Address: ....
Phone: ....
Email: ....
#Table: ....

Invitation sent?   YES ☐   NO ☐

NAME: ....

Address: ....
Phone: ....
Email: ....
#Table: ....

Invitation sent?   YES ☐   NO ☐

NAME: ....

Address: ....
Phone: ....
Email: ....
#Table: ....

Invitation sent?   YES ☐   NO ☐

NAME: ....

Address: ....
Phone: ....
Email: ....
#Table: ....

Invitation sent?   YES ☐   NO ☐

NAME: ....

Address: ....
Phone: ....
Email: ....
#Table: ....

Invitation sent?   YES ☐   NO ☐

NAME: ....

Address: ....
Phone: ....
Email: ....
#Table: ....

Invitation sent?   YES ☐   NO ☐

Personal Guest List

NAME: ....

Address: ....
Phone: ....
Email: ....
#Table: ....

Invitation sent?   YES ☐   NO ☐

NAME: ....

Address: ....
Phone: ....
Email: ....
#Table: ....

Invitation sent?   YES ☐   NO ☐

NAME: ....

Address: ....
Phone: ....
Email: ....
#Table: ....

Invitation sent?   YES ☐   NO ☐

NAME: ....

Address: ....
Phone: ....
Email: ....
#Table: ....

Invitation sent?   YES ☐   NO ☐

NAME: ....

Address: ....
Phone: ....
Email: ....
#Table: ....

Invitation sent?   YES ☐   NO ☐

NAME: ....

Address: ....
Phone: ....
Email: ....
#Table: ....

Invitation sent?   YES ☐   NO ☐

NAME: ....

Address: ....
Phone: ....
Email: ....
#Table: ....

Invitation sent?   YES ☐   NO ☐

NAME: ....

Address: ....
Phone: ....
Email: ....
#Table: ....

Invitation sent?   YES ☐   NO ☐

Personal Guest List

NAME: ....

Address: ....
Phone: ....
Email: ....
#Table: ....

Invitation sent?   YES ☐   NO ☐

NAME: ....

Address: ....
Phone: ....
Email: ....
#Table: ....

Invitation sent?   YES ☐   NO ☐

NAME: ....

Address: ....
Phone: ....
Email: ....
#Table: ....

Invitation sent?   YES ☐   NO ☐

NAME: ....

Address: ....
Phone: ....
Email: ....
#Table: ....

Invitation sent?   YES ☐   NO ☐

NAME: ....

Address: ....
Phone: ....
Email: ....
#Table: ....

Invitation sent?   YES ☐   NO ☐

NAME: ....

Address: ....
Phone: ....
Email: ....
#Table: ....

Invitation sent?   YES ☐   NO ☐

NAME: ....

Address: ....
Phone: ....
Email: ....
#Table: ....

Invitation sent?   YES ☐   NO ☐

NAME: ....

Address: ....
Phone: ....
Email: ....
#Table: ....

Invitation sent?   YES ☐   NO ☐

Personal Guest List

NAME: ....

Address: ....
Phone: ....
Email: ....
#Table: ....

Invitation sent?   YES ⬜   NO ⬜

NAME: ....

Address: ....
Phone: ....
Email: ....
#Table: ....

Invitation sent?   YES ⬜   NO ⬜

NAME: ....

Address: ....
Phone: ....
Email: ....
#Table: ....

Invitation sent?   YES ⬜   NO ⬜

NAME: ....

Address: ....
Phone: ....
Email: ....
#Table: ....

Invitation sent?   YES ⬜   NO ⬜

NAME: ....

Address: ....
Phone: ....
Email: ....
#Table: ....

Invitation sent?   YES ⬜   NO ⬜

NAME: ....

Address: ....
Phone: ....
Email: ....
#Table: ....

Invitation sent?   YES ⬜   NO ⬜

NAME: ....

Address: ....
Phone: ....
Email: ....
#Table: ....

Invitation sent?   YES ⬜   NO ⬜

NAME: ....

Address: ....
Phone: ....
Email: ....
#Table: ....

Invitation sent?   YES ⬜   NO ⬜

Personal Guest List

NAME: ....

Address: ....
Phone: ....
Email: ....
#Table: ....

Invitation sent?   YES ☐   NO ☐

NAME: ....

Address: ....
Phone: ....
Email: ....
#Table: ....

Invitation sent?   YES ☐   NO ☐

NAME: ....

Address: ....
Phone: ....
Email: ....
#Table: ....

Invitation sent?   YES ☐   NO ☐

NAME: ....

Address: ....
Phone: ....
Email: ....
#Table: ....

Invitation sent?   YES ☐   NO ☐

NAME: ....

Address: ....
Phone: ....
Email: ....
#Table: ....

Invitation sent?   YES ☐   NO ☐

NAME: ....

Address: ....
Phone: ....
Email: ....
#Table: ....

Invitation sent?   YES ☐   NO ☐

NAME: ....

Address: ....
Phone: ....
Email: ....
#Table: ....

Invitation sent?   YES ☐   NO ☐

NAME: ....

Address: ....
Phone: ....
Email: ....
#Table: ....

Invitation sent?   YES ☐   NO ☐

Personal Guest List

NAME: ....

Address: ....
Phone: ....
Email: ....
#Table: ....

Invitation sent?   YES ⬭   NO ⬭

NAME: ....

Address: ....
Phone: ....
Email: ....
#Table: ....

Invitation sent?   YES ⬭   NO ⬭

NAME: ....

Address: ....
Phone: ....
Email: ....
#Table: ....

Invitation sent?   YES ⬭   NO ⬭

NAME: ....

Address: ....
Phone: ....
Email: ....
#Table: ....

Invitation sent?   YES ⬭   NO ⬭

NAME: ....

Address: ....
Phone: ....
Email: ....
#Table: ....

Invitation sent?   YES ⬭   NO ⬭

NAME: ....

Address: ....
Phone: ....
Email: ....
#Table: ....

Invitation sent?   YES ⬭   NO ⬭

NAME: ....

Address: ....
Phone: ....
Email: ....
#Table: ....

Invitation sent?   YES ⬭   NO ⬭

NAME: ....

Address: ....
Phone: ....
Email: ....
#Table: ....

Invitation sent?   YES ⬭   NO ⬭

Invitations

Invitations for Quinceañeras are important. They represent what will happen on the indicated date, the time the celebration will take place, and the place chosen for it. In addition to this, other types of information are also added to capture the attention of the people who are going to be invited so that they do not miss the party.

That is why it is very important that the invitations are presented in the best possible way. It can be given an creative and unique touch to match the theme in order to bring everything in harmony and unify the entire party.

Keep in mind that the invitations will be the first thing that the guests will see for your party so they must make a good impression on them so that they decide to attend your Quinceañera. If you don't know what invitations to make, we leave you several ideas, so read on to discover the Quinceañera invitation design that you like the most.

Invitation Checklist

Budget $ ....

Contact person: ....
Phone: ....
Email: ....

Cost $ ....

Save the date cards: ....
Envelopes: ....
RSVP cards: ....

Budget $ ....

Contact person: ....
Phone: ....
Email: ....

Cost $ ....

Save the date cards: ....
Envelopes: ....
RSVP cards: ....

Budget $ ....

Contact person: ....
Phone: ....
Email: ....

Cost $ ....

Save the date cards: ....
Envelopes: ....
RSVP cards: ....

Budget $ ....

Contact person: ....
Phone: ....
Email: ....

Cost $ ....

Save the date cards: ....
Envelopes: ....
RSVP cards: ....

Budget $ ....

Contact person: ....
Phone: ....
Email: ....

Cost $ ....

Save the date cards: ....
Envelopes: ....
RSVP cards: ....

Enjoy your big day!

Menu Planner

Fill out the details below to help make your Quince Menu.

Consider your budget and number of guests when planning the menu for your Quinceañera.

Do you have a theme for the food?   Yes ☐ _____ No ☐

Budget $_____   Cost $_____   Grand total $_____

How many guests will you have? _____ Adults: _____ Kids: _____

What kind of food do they like? _____ Allergies: _____ Vegan: _____

Type of Quince Menu:

Plated Sit-down ☐   Cocktail Style: ☐

Buffet Style: ☐   Stations: ☐

Family Style: ☐   Taquiza: ☐

Price per plate $_____

\# Of Courses: _____

Soup: _____   Salad: _____

Main Entree: _____

Proteins: _____ Sides: _____

Dessert: _____ Coffee: _____

Bar

Open Bar $: _____   What kind of drinks? _____

Cash Bar $: _____   _____

Reception $: _____   Glass or plastic cups? _____

Total Price $: _____   _____

Chef Ambrocio   f Chef Ambrocio   Chefambrocio

Final Menu

Appetizers

Soup & Salad

Bread & Tortila

Main Course

Sides

Desserts

Cake

Beverages

Treats & Snacks

Selection of Caterer

NAME: ....

Option 1.

Address: ....
Contact: ....
Email: ....
Price per person: ....
Date to schedule visit: ....
Notes: ....

....

NAME: ....

Option 2.

Address: ....
Contact: ....
Email: ....
Price per person: ....
Date to schedule visit: ....
Notes: ....

....

NAME: ....

Option 3.

Address: ....
Contact: ....
Email: ....
Price per person: ....
Date to schedule visit: ....
Notes: ....

....

NAME: ....

Option 4.

Address: ....
Contact: ....
Email: ....
Price per person: ....
Date to schedule visit: ....
Notes: ....

....

NAME: ....

Option 5.

Address: ....
Contact: ....
Email: ....
Price per person: ....
Date to schedule visit: ....
Notes: ....

....

NAME: ....

Option 6.

Address: ....
Contact: ....
Email: ....
Price per person: ....
Date to schedule visit: ....
Notes: ....

....

Cake

Make sure to choose a cake that matches your color or your theme.

What design would it have?

_____

What size would it be?

_____

How will it get to the venue?

_____

Cake Checklist

Cake Budget

Price: ....

# of guests: ....

Cake shop: ....

Phone: ....

Style of Cake

- ☐ Traditional
- ☐ Contemporary
- ☐ Dramatic
- ☐ Ornate
- ☐ Simple
- ☐ Regal
- ☐ Unique

Flavors

- ☐ Chocolate
- ☐ Mocha
- ☐ Truffle
- ☐ Mousse
- ☐ Caramel
- ☐ Orange
- ☐ Other

Decorations

- ☐ Fresh flowers
- ☐ Piping
- ☐ Cake Top
- ☐ Pearls
- ☐ Gold or silver leaf
- ☐ Chocolate shavings
- ☐ Sugar flowers
- ☐ Other

Colors

- ☐ Peach
- ☐ Yellow
- ☐ Red
- ☐ Pink
- ☐ Lavender
- ☐ Write
- ☐ Other

Structure

- ☐ Road
- ☐ Oval
- ☐ Rectangular
- ☐ Other

Surprise Dance

The surprise dance is the most exciting part of the Quinceañera. These tips can help plan your surprise dance:

1. Decide the song
2. Choose the outfits
3. Contact choreographer
4. Select the music style

Style

Bachata, Salsa, Merengue, Pop, Rock

SONG SELECTION

Song title: _____

Song artist: _____

SCHEDULE PRACTICE WITH YOUR COURT

Practice: _____

Date: _____

Time: _____

Place: _____

DANCE STUDIO/CHOREOGRAPHER

Name: _____

Phone Number: _____

Address: _____

Music

You can pick from:

- DJ
- Live band
- Mariachi

What music would you like for dinner time?_____

What kind of music do your guests like? _____

Give your DJ a list of music that you would like to ensure is played.

DJ CHECKLIST

- Make sure DJ has experience working with Quinceañeras
- Professional DJ
- Versatile DJ: plays all kinds of music
- Has a professional equipment
- Willing to plan the hours of your party in order to choose the right music for each moment.
- Has gadgets for entertaining, such as robot, balloons, lights, etc.
- Ask for samples of their work.
- Get recommendations and referrals.

Pro DJ
Alexander Ozmar

Pro DJ Company   www.prodjcompany.com

DJ/Music

DJ/Musical Group/Entertainment: _____

Phone: _____   Company: _____

E-mail: _____   Address: _____

Start Time: _____   End time: _____

Summary of the entertainment service: _____
_____
_____
_____
_____

Estimated price: _____

INCLUDES:	YES	NO	COST
Stereo:	◯	◯	_____
Lights:	◯	◯	_____
Special effects:	◯	◯	_____
Money tip:	◯	◯	_____

TOTAL COST: _____

NOTES: _____
_____
_____
_____
_____

Photography

Tips for Quinceañeras from ER Studio:

When choosing a photographer, researching their work is very important but creating a bond and building trust will yield better results. The photographer and the Quinceañera should vibe to connect ideas and deliver a unique view tailored for every individual.

For your photoshoot, it's always important to care beyond your face. We all know that hair and makeup should be done by a professional but one often overlooked aspect is dry skin on your arms, elbows, and neck. No one wants chipped nails, dry arms or ashy elbows so remember to pay attention to other details!

To make your experience more enjoyable and help your photographer make the most of the day, communication is key! Let your photographer in on the details of your day, any surprises that might be planned and personal info that might influence the structure of the day. After all, the photographer will be by your side all day and you don't want lack of communication to create a roadblock in creativity.

Photography
Eduardo Rodriguez

 ER Studio   ER Studio

Vendors Contact Sheet

Quince Emergency Bag:

It's very important for you to enjoy your big day, which means having a Quince Emergency Bag to avoid any mishaps. Make sure to give it to someone that will be with you throughout the day.

CHECKLIST:

- ☐ Contacts
- ☐ Eyeglasses
- ☐ Extra Makeup
- ☐ Sewing Kit
- ☐ Deodorant/Perfume
- ☐ Snacks/Water
- ☐ Tissues
- ☐ Bobby Pins
- ☐ Safety Pins
- ☐ Hairspray
- ☐ Mints
- ☐ Tampons/Pads
- ☐ Phone Charger
- ☐ Bug Spray
- ☐ Flats
- ☐ Advil/Tylenol
- ☐ Other _____

Day of

TODAY'S THE BIG DAY!

ARE YOU READY? DON'T BE NERVOUS. EVERYTHING YOU HAVE WRITTEN DOWN AND PLANNED FOR IS FINALLY COMING TO LIFE! THE MONTHS OF PLANNING YOUR QUINCE HAVE COME TO AN END AND NOW IT'S TIME TO ENJOY YOUR DAY!

My Magic Day Timeline

Hair and Makeup

Get Dressed

Church Ceremony

Picture Time

Your Guests Arrive

Grand Entrance

Toast

Dinner

Change of Shoes & Last Doll

Father-Daughter Dance

Quince Waltz/Suprise Dance

Cake Cutting

Time to Party

Important Contacts

NAME: ....

Phone Number: ....

NAME: ....

Phone Number: ....

NAME: ....

Phone Number: ....

NAME: ....

Phone Number: ....

NAME: ....

Phone Number: ....

NAME: ....

Phone Number: ....

NAME: ....

Phone Number: ....

NAME: ....

Phone Number: ....

NAME: ....

Phone Number: ....

NAME: ....

Phone Number: ....

NAME: ....

Phone Number: ....

NAME: ....

Phone Number: ....

NAME: ....

Phone Number: ....

NAME: ....

Phone Number: ....

NAME: ....

Phone Number: ....

NAME: ....

Phone Number: ....

Important Contacts

NAME: ....

Phone Number: ....

NAME: ....

Phone Number: ....

NAME: ....

Phone Number: ....

NAME: ....

Phone Number: ....

NAME: ....

Phone Number: ....

NAME: ....

Phone Number: ....

NAME: ....

Phone Number: ....

NAME: ....

Phone Number: ....

NAME: ....

Phone Number: ....

NAME: ....

Phone Number: ....

NAME: ....

Phone Number: ....

NAME: ....

Phone Number: ....

NAME: ....

Phone Number: ....

NAME: ....

Phone Number: ....

NAME: ....

Phone Number: ....

NAME: ....

Phone Number: ....

Important Contacts

NAME: ....

Phone Number: ....

NAME: ....

Phone Number: ....

NAME: ....

Phone Number: ....

NAME: ....

Phone Number: ....

NAME: ....

Phone Number: ....

NAME: ....

Phone Number: ....

NAME: ....

Phone Number: ....

NAME: ....

Phone Number: ....

NAME: ....

Phone Number: ....

NAME: ....

Phone Number: ....

NAME: ....

Phone Number: ....

NAME: ....

Phone Number: ....

NAME: ....

Phone Number: ....

NAME: ....

Phone Number: ....

NAME: ....

Phone Number: ....

NAME: ....

Phone Number: ....

Important Contacts

NAME: ....

Phone Number: ....

NAME: ....

Phone Number: ....

NAME: ....

Phone Number: ....

NAME: ....

Phone Number: ....

NAME: ....

Phone Number: ....

NAME: ....

Phone Number: ....

NAME: ....

Phone Number: ....

NAME: ....

Phone Number: ....

NAME: ....

Phone Number: ....

NAME: ....

Phone Number: ....

NAME: ....

Phone Number: ....

NAME: ....

Phone Number: ....

NAME: ....

Phone Number: ....

NAME: ....

Phone Number: ....

NAME: ....

Phone Number: ....

NAME: ....

Phone Number: ....

Your QUINCEAÑERA IS ONE OF THE MOST IMPORTANT TRADITIONS IN YOUR LIFE. ENJOY YOUR DAY, HAVE FUN, AND CREATE UNFORGETTABLE MEMORIES.

January

Date:_____

Sunday	Monday	Tuesday	Wednesday	Thursday	Friday	Saturday

Don't forget to do

- [ ] ....
- [ ] ....
- [ ] ....
- [ ] ....
- [ ] ....
- [ ] ....
- [ ] ....
- [ ] ....
- [ ] ....
- [ ] ....

Notes

February

Date:_____

Sunday	Monday	Tuesday	Wednesday	Thursday	Friday	Saturday

Don't forget to do

- ☐ ....
- ☐ ....
- ☐ ....
- ☐ ....
- ☐ ....
- ☐ ....
- ☐ ....
- ☐ ....
- ☐ ....
- ☐ ....

Notes

March

Date:_____

Sunday	Monday	Tuesday	Wednesday	Thursday	Friday	Saturday

Don't forget to do

- [ ]
- [ ]
- [ ]
- [ ]
- [ ]
- [ ]
- [ ]
- [ ]
- [ ]
- [ ]

Notes

April

Date:_____

Sunday	Monday	Tuesday	Wednesday	Thursday	Friday	Saturday

Don't forget to do

- ☐ _____
- ☐ _____
- ☐ _____
- ☐ _____
- ☐ _____
- ☐ _____
- ☐ _____
- ☐ _____
- ☐ _____
- ☐ _____

Notes

May

Date:_____

Sunday	Monday	Tuesday	Wednesday	Thursday	Friday	Saturday

Don't forget to do

- [ ] ....
- [ ] ....
- [ ] ....
- [ ] ....
- [ ] ....
- [ ] ....
- [ ] ....
- [ ] ....
- [ ] ....
- [ ] ....

Notes

June

Date:_____

Sunday	Monday	Tuesday	Wednesday	Thursday	Friday	Saturday

Don't forget to do

- [ ]
- [ ]
- [ ]
- [ ]
- [ ]
- [ ]
- [ ]
- [ ]
- [ ]

Notes

July

Date:_____

Sunday	Monday	Tuesday	Wednesday	Thursday	Friday	Saturday

Don't forget to do

- ☐ ....
- ☐ ....
- ☐ ....
- ☐ ....
- ☐ ....
- ☐ ....
- ☐ ....
- ☐ ....
- ☐ ....

Notes

August

Date:_____

Sunday	Monday	Tuesday	Wednesday	Thursday	Friday	Saturday

Don't forget to do

- [ ] ....
- [ ] ....
- [ ] ....
- [ ] ....
- [ ] ....
- [ ] ....
- [ ] ....
- [ ] ....
- [ ] ....

Notes

September

Date:_____

Sunday	Monday	Tuesday	Wednesday	Thursday	Friday	Saturday

Don't forget to do

- ☐
- ☐
- ☐
- ☐
- ☐
- ☐
- ☐
- ☐
- ☐
- ☐

Notes

October

Date:_____

Sunday	Monday	Tuesday	Wednesday	Thursday	Friday	Saturday

Don't forget to do

- ☐ ....
- ☐ ....
- ☐ ....
- ☐ ....
- ☐ ....
- ☐ ....
- ☐ ....
- ☐ ....
- ☐ ....

Notes

November

Date:_____

Sunday	Monday	Tuesday	Wednesday	Thursday	Friday	Saturday

Don't forget to do

- ☐ ....
- ☐ ....
- ☐ ....
- ☐ ....
- ☐ ....
- ☐ ....
- ☐ ....
- ☐ ....
- ☐ ....
- ☐ ....

Notes

December

Date:_____

Sunday	Monday	Tuesday	Wednesday	Thursday	Friday	Saturday

Don't forget to do

- ☐ ....
- ☐ ....
- ☐ ....
- ☐ ....
- ☐ ....
- ☐ ....
- ☐ ....
- ☐ ....
- ☐ ....

Notes

Notes

Notes

Beatriz Cantu

Publisher-Life Coach-Motivational Speaker-Event Organizer-Award Winning Author.

An influential motivational speaker and community leader who empowers youth by offering guidance on how to reach one's personal, professional, and academic goals. A passionate visionary and respected entrepreneur with over 11 years of experience, and award-winning author award-winning Author.

Mrs. Cantu is the founder and director of Sweet 15 Magazine, which was launched in Winter 2011. It aims to help Hispanic families plan their young daughter's quinceañera. In addition to the magazine, Mrs. Cantu accepted the role as the international director for the Plexon Group's Expo 15 & Sweet 16. This organization brings over 600 people and helps family plan their big event. The Expo offers a variety of businesses and services all in one location.